GASTRO BLAST

MAKE TASTY TREATS & LEARN GREAT SCIENCE

Comics, quizzes and questions answered! Get ready to make science delicious!

AMANDA McNEICE, VICTORIA STEVENSON AND
THE BRAIN POWER TEAM

FORMAC PUBLISHING COMPANY LIMITED

Copyright © 2016 by Brain Power Studio Inc.
All rights reserved. No part of this book may be reproduced or transmitted in any form or by any means, electronic or mechanical, including photocopying, or by any information storage or retrieval system, without permission in writing from the publisher.

Formac Publishing Company Limited recognizes the support of the Province of Nova Scotia through Nova Scotia Business Inc. We are pleased to work in partnership with the Province to develop and promote our creative industries of Nova Scotia. We acknowledge the support of the Canada Council for the Arts, which last year invested $153 million to bring the arts to Canadians throughout the country. This project has been made possible in part by the Government of Canada.

Cover design: Meghan Collins

Library and Archives Canada Cataloguing in Publication

McNeice, Amanda, 1983-, author
    Gastro blast : make tasty treats & learn great science : comics, quizzes and questions answered! Get ready to make science delicious! / Amanda McNeice, Victoria Stevenson and the Brain Power Team.

Includes index.
"Comics, quizzes and questions answered! Get ready to make science delicious".
ISBN 978-1-4595-0462-2 (paperback)

    1. Cooking--Juvenile literature. 2. Science--Experiments--Juvenile literature. 3. Cookbooks. I. Stevenson, Victoria, 1972-, author II. Brain Power Studio, author III. Title. IV. Title: Gastro blast (Television program)

TX714.M356 2016   j641.5'123   C2016-902060-6

Formac Publishing Company Limited
5502 Atlantic Street
Halifax, Nova Scotia, Canada
B3H 1G4
www.formac.ca

Printed and bound in Korea.

Credits

PRODUCED BY BRAIN POWER STUDIO / FORMAC PUBLISHING COMPANY LIMITED
EXECUTIVE PRODUCER: BETH STEVENSON
PROJECT MANAGER: HAYLEY DENNIS
PRODUCTION ASSISTANT: APRIL SNELL
GASTRO BLAST CREATED BY BETTY QUAN
INTRODUCING MICHAEL RUBINSTEIN AS LINK, EMILY AGARD AS I.Q. AND BOB STEVENSON AS GASTRO BOB
WRITTEN BY AMANDA MCNEICE AND VICTORIA STEVENSON
COMIC BOOKS ILLUSTRATIONS BY JEFF WASSON

PHOTOGRAPHY CREDITS

CHARACTER, INGREDIENT AND PROCESS PHOTOGRAPHS BY STAN YAVORSKIY
WWW.YAVORSKIYSTUDIO.COM
FINAL DISH PHOTOGRAPHS BY BONNIE PENNY PHOTOGRAPHY
WWW.BONNIEPENNY.CA

Contents

APPLE OATMEAL PANCAKES	4
BUTTERMILK BISCUITS	8
CHICKEN FINGERS	14
CHICKEN POT PIE	20
CHOCOLATE ZUCCHINI BREAD	26
DEVILLED EGGS	30
EMPANADAS	34
FISH TACOS	40
FRENCH ONION SOUP	44
GRANOLA AND GRANOLA BARS	48
GUACAMOLE AND BAKED TORTILLA CHIPS	54
LEMON MERINGUE PIE	58
MACARONI AND CHEESE	62
MANGO MOUSSE WITH PINEAPPLE JELLY	66
MINESTRONE SOUP	70
PICKLED CARROTS AND DILL PICKLES	74
PIZZA	78
SPAGHETTI WITH TOMATO SAUCE	82
STRAWBERRY SHORTCAKE	86
STUFFED BAKED POTATO SKINS	90
SUSHI VEGETABLE ROLLS	94
TOSSED GREEN SALAD WITH 3 SALAD DRESSINGS	98
TZATZIKI WITH HOMEMADE YOGURT	102
VEGETARIAN SLOPPY JOES AND MARINATED ZUCCHINI SALAD	106
VEGGIE LASAGNA AND RICOTTA CHEESE	110
WHOLE WHEAT BREAD	116
INDEX	120

Apple Oatmeal Pancakes

let's make some!

We'll learn about leavening agents!

Serves 4 to 6.
Adult needed: Yes
Hands-on time: 20 minutes
Total time: 20 minutes

✓ YOUR CHECKLIST!

✓ KITCHEN GEAR
- ◯ Measuring cups
- ◯ Measuring spoons
- ◯ Small bowl
- ◯ Large bowl
- ◯ Large spoon
- ◯ Frying pan
- ◯ Spatula

✓ INGREDIENTS
1. ◯ 1/4 cup (60 mL) all-purpose flour
2. ◯ 1/4 cup (60 mL) whole wheat flour
3. ◯ 1 tsp (5 mL) baking powder
4. ◯ 1/2 tsp (2 mL) ground cinnamon
5. ◯ 1/2 tsp (2 mL) fine sea salt
6. ◯ 1 1/4 cups (310 mL) large-flake rolled oats
7. ◯ 1 medium apple, grated, and core discarded
8. ◯ 1 cup (250 mL) plain yogurt
9. ◯ 1 cup (250 mL) 2% milk
10. ◯ 1 Tbsp (15 mL) honey
11. ◯ 2 large eggs, beaten
12. ◯ 2 Tbsp (30 mL) melted butter
13. ◯ Vegetable oil
14. ◯ Maple syrup for serving

Apple Oatmeal Pancakes

MAKE IT!

1. Combine the flours, baking powder, cinnamon and salt in a small bowl. Set aside.

2. Stir together the rolled oats, grated apple, yogurt, milk and honey in a large bowl.

3. Mix the beaten eggs and melted butter into the bowl of wet ingredients.

4. Add the dry ingredients and mix until just combined.

5. Heat a large frying pan over medium heat. Add a splash of vegetable oil in the pan.

6. Scoop batter using a 1/4 cup (60 mL) measure onto the hot frying pan.

7

Cook for 2 to 3 minutes or until the bottoms begin to brown and the bubbles on top begin to pop. Flip and cook for 2 minutes more or until the second side is browned. Repeat with the remaining batter. Serve hot with maple syrup.

Dear I.Q. . . .

Q. I wanted to bake light, fluffy pancakes for my mom, but they turned out hard and rubbery like I'd made Frisbees for my brother. I followed the recipe exactly, so what's going on? Should I add something else? Should I cook the pancakes longer? Help!

— Pouting about Pancakes in Petawawa

Dear Pouting,

Don't let a failed recipe get you down. You can solve the problem with science!

First, this recipe uses baking powder as a leavening agent to help the dough rise. Be sure the baking powder is still active and not stale: pour a bit of hot tap water in a bowl, add a half teaspoon of the powder and check to see if it fizzes. It should; that's the base and acid reacting and letting off some CO_2 gas. The CO_2 makes air spaces in the batter, so as the pancake cooks on the griddle, you should see a lot of bubbles!

Second, don't stir the mixture a lot. Make sure you only stir enough after adding the wet ingredients to moisten and blend with the dry ingredients. It's okay to have clumps in your pancake dough, but if you overmix, gluten will start to form from the proteins in the flour, and you'll end up with chewy dough — fine for pizza crust, but not what you're looking for in pancakes!

So remember, when you're making pancakes, always use an active leavening agent and a light hand when mixing for perfect results.

— Yours in food & science,
I.Q.

Buttermilk Biscuits

let's make some!

We'll learn about carbon dioxide!

Makes 12.
Adult needed: Yes
Hands-on time: 10 minutes
Total time: 20 minutes

✓ YOUR CHECKLIST!

✓ KITCHEN GEAR

- ◯ Large baking sheet
- ◯ Parchment paper
- ◯ Sifter
- ◯ Large bowl
- ◯ Measuring cups
- ◯ Measuring spoons
- ◯ 2 butter knives or a pastry cutter
- ◯ Large spoon
- ◯ Floured board
- ◯ Rolling pin
- ◯ Round 2" (5 cm) cookie cutter

✓ INGREDIENTS

1. ◯ 2 cups (500 mL) all-purpose flour, plus a little extra for the work surface
2. ◯ 1/2 tsp (2 mL) baking soda
3. ◯ 1/2 tsp (2 mL) fine sea salt
4. ◯ 1/4 cup (60 mL) cold butter, cubed
5. ◯ 1 cup (250 mL) buttermilk (approximate)

Buttermilk Biscuits

MAKE IT!

1. Preheat the oven to 450° F (230° C). Line a large baking sheet with parchment paper. Sift the flour into a large bowl.

2. Sift the baking soda and salt into the flour.

3. Working quickly and using a light touch, incorporate the butter using 2 butter knives (or a pastry cutter or your fingers) until the largest pieces of the mixture are the size of peas.

4. Add the buttermilk, stirring until the dough leaves the side of the bowl.

5. The dough should be slightly sticky. If the dough is too dry, add up to 2 Tbsp (30 mL) buttermilk.

6. Knead the dough on a lightly floured board, 5 times or until the dough comes together.

Roll out the dough, using a floured rolling pin, to a thickness of about 1 inch (2.5 cm).

Cut dough into 2 inch (5 cm) rounds with a cookie cutter or a straight-sided glass. Gently press the remaining scraps together and cut out a few more circles, if possible.

Transfer the biscuits to the baking sheet, making sure the biscuits don't touch each other. Bake for 12 minutes or until the biscuits begin to turn golden. Serve warm.

Flip to the next page so we can hop in this batter to find out what's going on!

Who knew your recipe was so scientific?

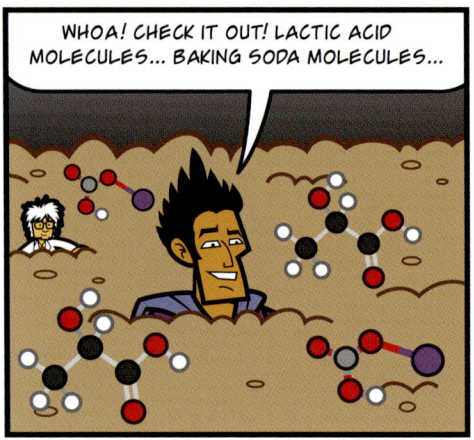
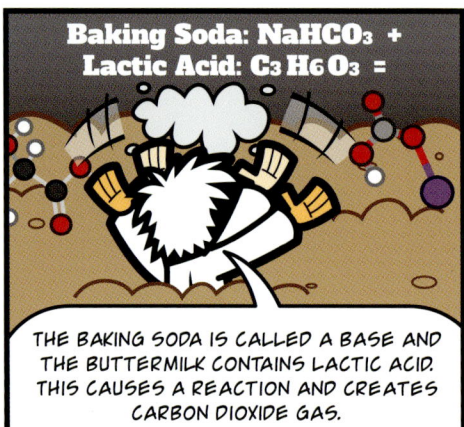

Variations/Tips

· For a sweet biscuit (for example, in the Strawberry Shortcake recipe on page 86), sprinkle the tops of the unbaked biscuits generously with granulated sugar.

· Add 1/4 cup (60 mL) golden raisins or dried currants to the dry ingredients and continue with the recipe.

· For a savoury biscuit, add 1/4 cup (60 mL) finely chopped fresh chives and 1/2 cup (125 mL) grated cheddar cheese.

· For even fluffier biscuits, add 2 tsp (10 mL) baking powder to the dry ingredients.

· Buttermilk is a low-fat milk that has had a culture added to it. If you can't find buttermilk in your grocery store, simply add 1 tsp (5 mL) white vinegar or lemon juice to 1 cup (250 mL) milk and stir. Let stand for 5 minutes before using.

Chicken Fingers

let's make some!

We'll learn about bacteria!

Serves 6 to 8.
Adult needed: Yes
Hands-on time: 20 minutes
Total time: 35 minutes

✓ YOUR CHECKLIST!

✓ KITCHEN GEAR

- ◯ Large baking sheet
- ◯ Food processor
- ◯ Measuring cups
- ◯ 3 medium bowls
- ◯ Measuring spoons
- ◯ Whisk
- ◯ Paper towels
- ◯ Pastry brush
- ◯ Spatula
- ◯ Fork and knife
- ◯ Tinfoil

✓ INGREDIENTS

1. ◯ 1 loaf whole-grain bread (or 3 cups [750 mL] store-bought whole-grain bread crumbs)
2. ◯ 3 large eggs
3. ◯ 1/2 cup (125 mL) 2% milk
4. ◯ 1 cup (250 mL) whole wheat flour
5. ◯ 1 tsp (5 mL) fine sea salt
6. ◯ 1/2 tsp (2 mL) freshly ground black pepper
7. ◯ 1/2 tsp (2 mL) paprika
8. ◯ 2 lbs (1 kg) boneless, skinless chicken breasts, sliced into long, thin pieces
9. ◯ Vegetable oil

Chicken Fingers 15

MAKE IT!

1. Place the baking tray in the oven to preheat at 425° F (220° C). Tear the loaf of bread up into smaller pieces, and place in a food processor.

2. Process the bread until it turns into fine bread crumbs. Place about 3 cups (750 mL) of the bread crumbs into a medium bowl and reserve any remaining crumbs for another recipe.

3. Whisk the eggs and milk together in a medium bowl.

4. Place the flour, salt, pepper and paprika in a third medium bowl.

5. Pat the strips of chicken dry with a paper towel. Roll the chicken pieces, a few at a time, in the flour mixture, until completely covered.

6. Place the chicken pieces in the egg mixture, being sure to cover the chicken with the egg mixture completely.

Remove the chicken pieces from the egg mixture and roll in the bread crumbs. Repeat with the remaining chicken pieces.

Carefully remove the baking sheet from the oven and generously brush with oil.

Place the chicken pieces on the oiled pan and return to the oven immediately. Bake for 10 minutes.

Remove the sheet from the oven and flip each piece of chicken over to bake the other side. Return the sheet to the oven and bake for another 5 minutes or until the chicken is golden brown and cooked through.

To test the chicken, use a fork and knife to slice into one of the larger pieces to make sure the chicken is white and the juices run clear. Serve with your favourite dipping sauce — ranch, honey-mustard or barbecue are tasty choices!

Get rid of that salmonella!

Chicken Pot Pie

let's make some!

We'll learn about steam!

Serves 8.
Adult needed: Yes
Hands-on time: 30 minutes
Total time: 1 hour 30 minutes

✓ YOUR CHECKLIST!

✓ KITCHEN GEAR

- ○ Measuring cups
- ○ Large saucepan
- ○ Wooden spoon
- ○ Measuring spoons
- ○ 9" x 2" (23 cm x 5 cm) deep dish
- ○ Fork
- ○ Whisk
- ○ Pastry brush
- ○ Knife

✓ INGREDIENTS

1. ○ 1/4 cup (60 mL) butter
2. ○ 3/4 cup (180 mL) finely chopped onions
3. ○ 1 1/2 cups (375 mL) finely chopped celery
4. ○ 1/4 cup (60 mL) all-purpose flour
5. ○ 1 1/4 cups (310 mL) chicken stock, hot
6. ○ 3/4 tsp (4 mL) fine sea salt
7. ○ 1/4 tsp (1 mL) freshly ground black pepper
8. ○ 2 Tbsp + 1 Tbsp (30 mL + 15 mL) 2% milk
9. ○ 3/4 lb (375 g) cooked boneless, skinless chicken breasts, cut into bite-sized pieces
10. ○ 3/4 cup (180 mL) chopped carrots, parboiled (see note on page 25)
11. ○ 3/4 cup (180 mL) frozen peas
12. ○ Two 9" (22.5 cm) store-bought pie crusts
13. ○ 1 large egg

Chicken Pot Pie 21

MAKE IT!

Preheat the oven to 375° F (190° C). Melt the butter in a large saucepan over medium heat.

Add the onions and celery.

Cook until soft, about 10 minutes.

Add the flour.

Cook over low heat for about 3 minutes, stirring often with a wooden spoon. (This is a roux made with onions and celery.)

Slowly add the hot chicken stock, salt and pepper to the roux and bring to a boil. Reduce the heat to low and simmer for about 5 minutes. Add 2 Tbsp (30 mL) milk.

22   Gastro Blast

Add the chicken, carrots and peas.

Stir until combined.

Line a 9 inch (22.5 cm) deep-dish pie plate with one pie shell. Fill the shell with the chicken filling.

Top the filling with the second crust. Use a fork to press and seal the edges closed.

Whisk the egg and 1 Tbsp (15 mL) milk together to make an egg wash, and brush this on the top crust. Cut small slits in the top crust to let the steam escape.

Bake for about 45 minutes or until the pie is golden brown and starting to bubble. Let the pie sit for about 15 minutes before serving.

Should you open the trap door?

What is PARBOILING? To parboil is to partially cook a food in boiling water. To parboil the carrots for this recipe, bring a small saucepan of water to a boil. Add the sliced carrots and boil for 2 minutes. Drain the carrots and continue on with your recipe.

Chocolate Zucchini Bread

let's make some!

We'll learn about fruits vs. veggies!

Makes 12 servings.
Adult needed: Yes
Hands-on time: 15 minutes
Total time: 1 hour

✓ YOUR CHECKLIST!

✓ KITCHEN GEAR

- 8" x 4" (20 cm x 10 cm) loaf pan
- Measuring cups
- Measuring spoons
- Large spoon
- Medium bowl
- Large bowl
- Whisk
- Rubber spatula
- Baking rack
- Plastic wrap (optional)

✓ INGREDIENTS

1. 3/4 cup (180 mL) all-purpose flour
2. 1/2 cup (125 mL) whole wheat flour
3. 1/4 cup (60 mL) cocoa powder
4. 1/2 tsp (2 mL) fine sea salt
5. 1/2 tsp (2 mL) baking powder
6. 1/2 tsp (2 mL) baking soda
7. 2 eggs
8. 1/2 cup (125 mL) vegetable oil
9. 1 cup (250 mL) granulated sugar
10. 1 tsp (5 mL) pure vanilla extract
11. 1 cup (250 mL) grated zucchini (about 1 small zucchini)
12. 1/2 cup (125 mL) chocolate chips

Chocolate Zucchini Bread

MAKE IT!

Preheat the oven to 325° F (160° C). Butter and flour an 8" x 4" (20 cm x 10 cm) loaf pan (see Tip on next page). Sprinkle with a small amount of cocoa powder.

Stir together the flours, remaining cocoa powder, salt, baking powder and baking soda in a medium bowl. Set aside.

Beat together the eggs, oil, sugar and vanilla in a large bowl using a whisk.

Add the flour mixture to the egg mixture

Beat until just combined.

Fold the zucchini and chocolate chips into the batter using a rubber spatula.

7 Pour batter into the prepared pan. Bake for about 50 minutes or until a toothpick inserted into the centre of the loaf comes out clean. Set the pan on a baking rack to cool. Once cool, remove the zucchini bread from the pan. Slice and serve.

Variations/Tips

If you wrap any leftover chocolate zucchini bread in plastic wrap, it will keep for up to 3 days.

How to butter and flour a baking pan: Smear a thin layer of butter in the baking pan, covering it thoroughly and evenly. Place about 1/4 cup (60 mL) flour in the pan and shake the flour around from side to side until all of the butter has been covered by flour. Remove any excess flour.

True Or False?

Zucchinis are a vegetable containing only 10% water.

Answer

False: Zucchinis are actually an underripe fruit and they are bursting with water. Water makes up 95% of their weight.

Devilled Eggs

let's make some!

We'll learn about sulphur!

Makes 24.
Adult needed: Yes
Hands-on time: 10 minutes
Total time: 40 minutes

✓ YOUR CHECKLIST!

✓ KITCHEN GEAR
- ◯ Large saucepan
- ◯ Measuring spoons
- ◯ Measuring cups
- ◯ Serving plate
- ◯ Hand mixer
- ◯ Medium bowl
- ◯ Squeeze Bag

✓ INGREDIENTS
1. ◯ 1/2 tsp + 1/4 tsp (2 mL + 1 mL) fine sea salt
2. ◯ 12 large eggs
3. ◯ 3/4 cup (180 mL) mayonnaise
4. ◯ 1 tsp (5 mL) fresh lemon juice (bottled lemon juice is also fine)
5. ◯ 1/2 tsp (2 mL) paprika (approximate)

MAKE IT!

Gently place the eggs in the bottom of a large saucepan. Cover the eggs with 1 inch (2.5 cm) of cold water mixed with 1/2 tsp (2 mL) fine sea salt.

Bring the water to a boil, remove the pan from the burner and cover the pan with a lid. Let the eggs sit for 10 minutes before draining the water and refilling the pot with cold water. Let the eggs cool for an additional 20 minutes.

Carefully peel the eggs (see Tip on next page). Cut the eggs in half, lengthwise. Scoop out the yolks and place in a medium bowl. Place the egg whites on a serving plate.

Add the mayonnaise, lemon juice and 1/4 tsp (1 mL) salt to the yolks. Beat with a hand mixer until smooth.

Squeeze the yolk mixture back into the egg whites.

Sprinkle a tiny amount of paprika on each devilled egg. Cover and refrigerate. Serve chilled.

Dear I.Q. . . . no green eggs for me!

Variations/Tips

How to peel hard-boiled eggs: *When the eggs have been cooked and cooled, drain off some of the water, leaving enough in the pan to just barely cover the eggs. Shake the saucepan with the eggs and water in it, hard enough to break the shells on the eggs. The water will get in between the shell and the eggs, making them easier to peel. Drain off the rest of the water and peel the eggs.*

Q: My dad and I thought it would be cool to have devilled eggs at our family picnic. We weren't sure how long to boil the eggs, so we cooked one as a test. When it was cool enough to crack open, it smelled stinky, kind of swampy, and even had a green ring in the middle! Hey, I like Dr. Seuss as much as the next kid, but stinky, green eggs are going to spoil our picnic. So break it to me I.Q., do we have to skip the devilled eggs or is there a better way to hard-boil an egg?

— Hard-Boiled in Hamilton

Dear Hard-Boiled,
Never fear, you won't have to give up your Devilled Egg dish and you won't have to hand out nose plugs at the picnic table either! The solution is simple — and it's science.

What you need is a timer. My guess is you and your dad probably let that egg sit in the pot way too long just to make sure it was cooked through. But guess what? If you overheat eggs, the hydrogen and sulphur in the egg white combines to form a smelly, sulphurous gas, and they also react with the iron compounds in the yellow yolk to make that green ring.

So how long you should boil those eggs depends on a few things — like how many are in the pot and their size. A good rule of thumb is to cover those eggs by at least an inch (2.5 cm) of cold water in a pot, bring them to a boil, turn off the heat, cover with a lid and let the eggs sit for 10 minutes. Remove them and fill the pot with cold water as soon as your timer goes off, and let the eggs cool for 20 minutes. That will help cut off the gas supply and cut down on the smell. So don't pass on the eggs, pass the eggs please!

— Yours in food & science,
I.Q.

Devilled Eggs 33

empanadas
let's make some!

We'll learn about laminates!

Serves 8.
Adult needed: Yes
Hands-on time: 40 minutes
Total time: 1 hour 40 minutes

✓ YOUR CHECKLIST!

✓ KITCHEN GEAR
- ○ 2 butter knives
- ○ Measuring cups
- ○ Measuring spoons
- ○ Whisk
- ○ Medium bowl
- ○ Plastic wrap
- ○ Large frying pan
- ○ Spoon
- ○ Large baking sheet
- ○ Parchment paper
- ○ Rolling pin
- ○ Knife
- ○ Fork
- ○ 2 small bowls
- ○ Pastry brush
- ○ Cookie cutter

✓ FILLING
1. ○ 2 Tbsp (30 mL) olive oil
2. ○ 1 lb (500 g) lean ground beef
3. ○ 1/2 cup (125 mL) finely chopped onion
4. ○ 1/4 cup (60 mL) golden raisins
5. ○ 4 cloves garlic, minced
6. ○ 2 Tbsp (30 mL) tomato paste
7. ○ 2 Tbsp (30 mL) white vinegar
8. ○ 2 tsp (10 mL) ground cumin
9. ○ 1 tsp (5 mL) chili powder
10. ○ 1 tsp (5 mL) fine sea salt

✓ INGREDIENTS DOUGH
1. ○ 3 cups (750 mL) all-purpose flour, plus a little extra for the work surface
2. ○ 1 Tbsp (15 mL) baking powder
3. ○ 2 tsp (10 mL) granulated sugar
4. ○ 1/4 tsp (1 mL) fine sea salt
5. ○ 1/2 cup (125 mL) cold vegetable shortening, cut into cubes
6. ○ 1 large egg
7. ○ 3/4 cup (180 mL) water

✓ AFTER ASSEMBLY
1. ○ 1 large egg
2. ○ 1 Tbsp (15 mL) 2% milk

empanadas 35

MAKE IT!

1. To make the dough, combine the flour, baking powder, sugar and salt into a medium bowl.

2. Add the cold shortening.

3. Incorporate the shortening using 2 butter knives until the largest pieces of the mixture are the size of peas.

4. Whisk together the egg and water in a small bowl. Add the liquid to the dry ingredients.

5. Combine the ingredients until you can form a ball.

6. Wrap the dough in plastic wrap and refrigerate for 30 minutes.

To make the filling, heat the olive oil in a large frying pan over medium heat. Add the ground beef, onions, garlic and golden raisins and cook until the beef is cooked through, about 5 minutes. Add the tomato paste, white vinegar, cumin, chili powder and sea salt and continue cooking for a few more minutes. Set aside.

Preheat the oven to 425° F (220° C). Line a large baking sheet with parchment paper. Cut the dough into 8 equal wedges. Lightly flour a work surface and roll out the dough to 1/4 inch (0.5 cm) thick. Cut out the dough with a 6 inch (15 cm) diameter cookie cutter.

Place about 1/3 cup (80 mL) of the filling in the centre of the dough and fold the dough over in half to enclose the filling.

Use a fork to press and seal the edges closed. Place the sealed empanada on the prepared baking sheet. Continue with the remaining dough and filling.

Whisk the egg and milk together in a small bowl. Brush the tops of the empanadas with the egg wash. Bake the empanadas for about 30 minutes or until they are golden brown. Remove from the oven and let sit for about 10 minutes before serving.

How does it all stack up?

Fish Tacos

let's make some!

We'll learn about the Maillard reaction!

Serves 4 to 6.
Adult needed: Yes
Hands-on time: 30 minutes
Total time: 50 minutes

✓ YOUR CHECKLIST!

✓ KITCHEN GEAR
- ○ 2 medium bowls
- ○ Measuring cups
- ○ Measuring spoons
- ○ Fork
- ○ Plate
- ○ Large frying pan
- ○ Large spoon

✓ INGREDIENTS
1. ○ 1/2 cup (125 mL) Greek yogurt
2. ○ 1/4 cup (60 mL) mayonnaise
3. ○ 2 Tbsp (30 mL) fresh lime juice (bottled lime juice is also fine)
4. ○ 1/4 tsp + 1/4 tsp (1 mL + 1 mL) fine sea salt
5. ○ 1/4 cup + 1 Tbsp (60 mL + 15 mL) olive oil
6. ○ 1 1/2 tsp (8 mL) chili powder
7. ○ 1 tsp (5 mL) dried oregano
8. ○ 1/2 tsp (2 mL) ground cumin
9. ○ 1/4 cup (60 mL) roughly chopped fresh cilantro leaves
10. ○ 1 lb (500 g) any firm white-fleshed fish fillet, such as cod or haddock, cut into bite-sized pieces
11. ○ 8 corn or wheat tortillas
12. ○ 2 cups (500 mL) thinly sliced green cabbage
13. ○ 1 cup (250 mL) finely diced tomatoes
14. ○ 1/2 cup (125 mL) finely sliced green onions
15. ○ 1 lime cut into 8 wedges

Fish Tacos

MAKE IT!

1. Combine the Greek yogurt, mayonnaise, lime juice and sea salt in a medium bowl. Refrigerate the yogurt mixture until you are ready to assemble the tacos.

2. Combine 1/4 cup (60 mL) olive oil, chili powder, oregano, cumin and chopped cilantro in a medium bowl and mix well. This is the marinade.

3. Place the fish pieces in the marinade and turn the fish to coat well. Let the fish marinate for 20 minutes.

4. Drape each shell directly over two bars of your oven rack . Bake for 8 to 10 minutes or until crispy. Remove from the oven and place on a serving plate.

5. Heat 1 tablespoon (15 mL) olive oil in a large frying pan over medium-high heat. Place the marinated fish in the hot pan. Sprinkle the fish with 1/4 tsp (1 mL) salt and sauté until cooked through, about 5 minutes. Try not to break up the pieces of fish too much.

6. To assemble the tacos, fill each tortilla shell evenly with the cooked fish, cabbage, tomatoes and green onions.

Drizzle with the yogurt mixture.

Serve with lime wedges.

Why are these fish tacos so yummy?

When sugars and proteins combine and react under high heat, making new and delicious flavours in browned, cooked food, it is known as:

a) The Maillard Reaction
b) The duck effect
c) The mayonnaise reaction
d) Burnt

answer
a) The Maillard Reaction.

Fish Tacos

French Onion Soup

let's make some!

We'll learn about onion gas!

Serves 6.
Adult needed: Yes
Hands-on time: 55 minutes
Total time: 1 hour 15 minutes

✓ YOUR CHECKLIST!

✓ KITCHEN GEAR
- ○ Measuring cups
- ○ Measuring spoons
- ○ Large stock pot
- ○ Large spoon
- ○ Large baking sheet
- ○ Ladle
- ○ 6 soup bowls

✓ INGREDIENTS
1. ○ 2 Tbsp (30 mL) butter
2. ○ 2 Tbsp (30 mL) olive oil
3. ○ 4 or 5 large yellow onions, thinly sliced
4. ○ 4 cups (1 L) beef stock
5. ○ 4 cups (1 L) chicken stock
6. ○ Pinch of dried thyme
7. ○ 2 tsp (10 mL) sea salt
8. ○ 1/4 tsp (1 mL) freshly ground black pepper
9. ○ 6 thick slices French bread
10. ○ 1 1/2 cups (375 mL) combination of grated mozzarella and cheddar cheese

French Onion Soup

MAKE IT!

Heat the butter and olive oil in a large stock pot.

Add the sliced onions and cook over low heat until golden brown and caramelized, about 45 minutes or so.

Don't allow to burn. The onions should slowly turn a dark golden brown and have a sweet flavour.

Add the beef stock, chicken stock and thyme. Bring to a simmer and cook for 20 minutes.

Season with salt and pepper.

Preheat the broiler. Lay thick slices of French bread on a baking sheet and toast for a minute or so, until golden.

Cover each slice with the grated cheeses and return to the broiler until the cheese is melting and starting to bubble, a minute or so. Watch carefully!

Ladle the soup into 6 bowls. Place a cheesy toast on top of the soup in each bowl. Serve immediately.

What is causing all these tears?

Our eyes tear up when we're cutting onions, the key ingredient in this soup, because:

a) It's just such a beautiful soup.
b) We're sad about cutting the onion into small pieces.
c) The onion is dusty from growing in the ground.
d) Sulphur in the cells of the onion makes a sulphur-based gas that irritates our eyes.

answer

d) Sulphur in the cells of the onion makes a sulphur-based gas that irritates our eyes.

French Onion Soup

Granola and Granola Bars
let's make some!

We'll learn about binding agents!

Granola
Makes 4 cups (1 L).
Adult needed: Yes
Hands-on time: 10 minutes
Total time: 40 minutes

Granola Bars
Makes 12 bars.
Adult needed: Yes
Hands-on time: 20 minutes
Total time: 1 hour 20 minutes

✓ YOUR CHECKLIST!

✓ KITCHEN GEAR
- ○ Large baking sheet
- ○ Parchment paper
- ○ Measuring cups
- ○ Measuring spoons
- ○ Large bowl
- ○ Small saucepan
- ○ Large spoon
- ○ Airtight container

✓ INGREDIENTS
1. ○ 2 cups (500 mL) large-flake rolled oats
2. ○ 1/2 cup (125 mL) wheat germ
3. ○ 1/2 cup (125 mL) shredded unsweetened coconut
4. ○ 1/2 cup (125 mL) unsalted pumpkin seeds
5. ○ 1 Tbsp (15 mL) whole flax seeds
6. ○ 1/2 cup (125 mL) honey
7. ○ 1/4 cup (60 mL) coconut oil
8. ○ 1/2 tsp (2 mL) ground cinnamon
9. ○ 1 cup (250 mL) chopped dried apricots

GRANOLA

MAKE IT!

1. Preheat the oven to 350° F (175° C). Line a large baking sheet with parchment paper. Toss the oats, wheat germ, coconut, pumpkin seeds and flax seeds together in a large bowl. Set aside.

2. In a small saucepan, warm the honey, coconut oil and ground cinnamon over low heat until the oil has melted.

3. Pour the oil mixture over the dry ingredients and toss thoroughly.

4. Spread the granola mixture evenly on the prepared pan.

5. Bake for 25 to 30 minutes, stirring occasionally. The granola should be a dark golden colour.

6. Remove the granola from the oven and stir in the chopped dried apricots. Leave the granola to cool on the baking sheet. Break the granola up into little clumps. Store in an airtight container.

Who's the glue?

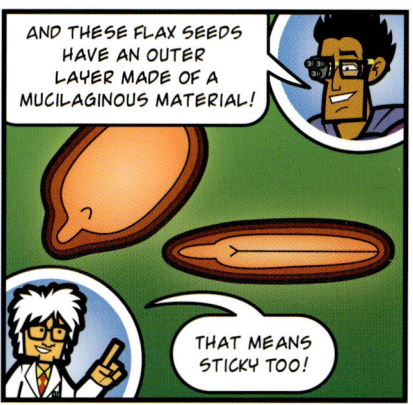

✓ YOUR CHECKLIST!

GRANOLA BARS

✓ KITCHEN GEAR
- ○ Measuring cups
- ○ Measuring spoons
- ○ 9" x 13" (23 cm x 33 cm) baking pan
- ○ Large bowl
- ○ Medium bowl
- ○ Small bowl
- ○ Parchment paper
- ○ Food processor
- ○ Small saucepan
- ○ Whisk
- ○ Spatula
- ○ Knife
- ○ Cutting board

✓ INGREDIENTS
1. ○ 1 cup (250 mL) chopped dried apricots
2. ○ 1/2 cup (125 mL) honey
3. ○ 1/4 cup (60 mL) coconut oil
4. ○ 1/2 tsp (2 mL) ground cinnamon
5. ○ 2 cups (500 mL) large-flake rolled oats
6. ○ 1/2 cup (125 mL) wheat germ
7. ○ 1/2 cup (125 mL) shredded unsweetened coconut
8. ○ 1/4 cup (60 mL) unsalted pumpkin seeds
9. ○ 1 Tbsp (15 mL) ground flax seeds
10. ○ 2 Tbsp (30 mL) water

52   Gastro Blast

MAKE IT!

1. Preheat the oven to 350 F (175 C). Place the chopped apricots in a medium bowl, and pour boiling water over them. Let soak for 30 minutes. Drain the apricots and place in a food processor. Purée until they are smooth.

2. Place the honey, coconut oil and cinnamon in a small saucepan. Heat the mixture over low heat until the oil is melted.

3. Combine the oats, wheat germ, coconut and pumpkin seeds together in a large bowl. In a small bowl, whisk the ground flax seeds and water together until it is the consistency of an egg white.

4. Pour the hot honey mixture over the dry ingredients, and stir well. Add the pureed apricots and flax seed mixture until throughly combined.

5. Using a spatula, press the granola mixture firmly into the prepared pan, making sure it is evenly distributed.

6. Bake for 25 to 30 minutes, until the granola has turned a dark golden colour. Remove from the oven and let cool for at least 1 hour. Slice into 12 bars. Store in an airtight container.

Guacamole and Baked Tortilla Chips

let's make some!

We'll learn about veggie browning and super villains too!

Guacamole
Makes 2 cups (500 mL).
Adult needed: No
Hands-on time: 10 minutes
Total time: 10 minutes

Baked Tortilla Chips
Makes about 8 dozen chips.
Adult needed: Yes
Hands-on time: 10 minutes
Total time: 25 minutes

✓ GUACAMOLE

✓ KITCHEN GEAR
- Knife
- Large spoon
- Large bowl
- Potato masher

✓ INGREDIENTS
1. 4 ripe avocados
2. 1/3 cup (80 mL) fresh lime juice (2 to 3 limes)
3. 1/2 cup (125 mL) finely sliced green onions
4. 3/4 cup (180 mL) diced fresh tomatoes
5. 3/4 tsp (4 mL) fine sea salt

✓ BAKED TORTILLA CHIPS

✓ KITCHEN GEAR
- Knife
- Cutting board
- Large baking sheet
- Parchment paper
- Tongs

✓ INGREDIENTS
1. One 8 oz (250 g) package fresh corn or whole wheat tortillas
2. 1/2 tsp (2 mL) fine sea salt, or to taste
3. Olive oil for brushing

MAKE IT – GUACAMOLE!

1. Slice the avocados in half.

2. Scoop out the flesh (see Tip on next page) and place in a large bowl.

3. Squeeze the lime juice into a container. Add the lime juice to the avocado.

4. Mash the avocado together with the juice using a potato masher until the mixture is a little more smooth than chunky.

Add the tomatoes, green onions and salt.

Taste for seasoning using a tortilla chip.

MAKE IT — BAKED TORTILLA CHIPS!

Preheat the oven to 350° F (175° C). Slice the tortillas into small triangles.

Spread the tortilla triangles out on the baking sheet in a single layer. Brush lightly with olive oil, and sprinkle with sea salt. Bake for 6 minutes.

Flip the triangles over and brush lightly with olive oil, and sprinkle with salt. Bake for another 6 to 10 minutes, or until the tortillas are starting to turn golden and get crispy.

Remove from the oven and let cool. Serve with guacamole or salsa.

Variations/Tips

- Guacamole is best eaten the day it's made. However, if you use enough lime juice, it will keep, covered in the refrigerator, for up to 2 days. The top of the guacamole will still oxidize, but you can either scrape that off or stir it in.

- Add 1/2 cup (125 mL) chopped fresh cilantro.

- Add half of a jalapeño pepper, finely diced.

How to Scoop an Avocado: Using a sharp paring knife, cut the avocado in half lengthwise. Remove the pit by prying it out with a dull knife or spoon. Using a large spoon, scoop all of the avocado flesh out of the skin and place the flesh in a large bowl. Discard the skins.

How to stop the oxygen?

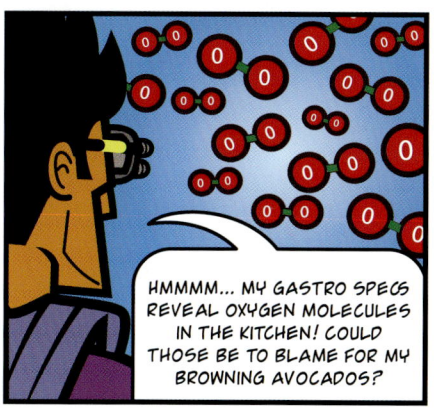

Lemon Meringue Pie

let's make some!

We'll learn about egg proteins!

Serves 8.
Adult needed: Yes
Hands-on time: 20 minutes
Total time: 8 hours or overnight

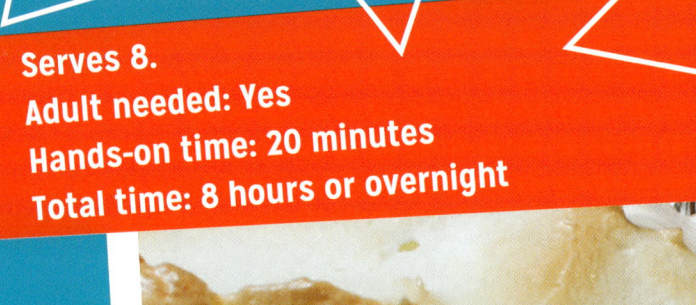

✓ YOUR CHECKLIST!

✓ KITCHEN GEAR
- ○ 2 medium bowls
- ○ Whisk
- ○ Hand mixer
- ○ Spoon

✓ INGREDIENTS
1. ○ One 14 oz (414 mL) can sweetened condensed milk
2. ○ 4 large eggs
3. ○ 1/2 cup + 2 Tbsp (125 mL + 30 mL) fresh lemon juice
4. ○ One 9" (22.5 cm) graham cracker crust, premade
5. ○ 1/4 tsp (1 mL) cream of tartar
6. ○ 1/4 cup (60 mL) granulated sugar

Lemon Meringue Pie

MAKE IT!

Preheat the oven to 350° F (175° C). Separate the egg yolks from the egg whites, being careful not to get any yolk in the whites. Refrigerate the egg whites until needed.

Whisk the sweetened condensed milk, egg yolks and lemon juice in a medium bowl until smooth.

Pour into the prepared pie crust. Bake for 15 minutes.

Remove from the oven and let cool.

Cover and refrigerate the pie for 8 hours or overnight.

Preheat the oven to 300° F (150° C). Place the egg whites into a clean bowl. Whip the egg whites until they get frothy.

Add the cream of tartar and the sugar, a little at a time. Continue beating until the whites form stiff peaks.

Spoon the meringue onto the chilled pie. Place the pie in the oven for 5 to 10 minutes, or until the meringue starts to turn golden around the edges – keep a close eye on it. Cool to room temperature and serve.

Can't they stay together?

You have to separate the egg whites from the yolk to make a meringue because:

a) It's fun to play with the egg shell cup.
b) Yolks are only for main dishes, not desserts.
c) The egg white proteins can't stretch and trap air if the fats (lipids) in the egg yolks mess with the protein network.
d) The egg white proteins are too watery when the yolks are added.

answer

c) The egg white proteins can't stretch and trap air if the fats (lipids) in the egg yolks mess with the protein network.

Lemon Meringue Pie

Macaroni and Cheese

let's make some!

We'll learn about starch!

Serves 10 to 12.
Adult needed: Yes
Hands-on time: 30 minutes
Total time: 1 hour

✓ YOUR CHECKLIST!

✓ KITCHEN GEAR
- ○ 9" x 13" (23 cm x 33 cm) baking pan
- ○ Medium saucepan
- ○ Large saucepan
- ○ Wooden spoon
- ○ Whisk

✓ INGREDIENTS
- **1** ○ 4 cups (1 L) 2% milk
- **2** ○ 1/2 cup (125 mL) butter
- **3** ○ 1/2 cup (125 mL) all-purpose flour
- **4** ○ 6 cups (1.5 L) grated cheddar cheese
- **5** ○ 2 tsp (10 mL) fine sea salt
- **6** ○ 1 tsp (5 mL) freshly ground black pepper
- **7** ○ 1 lb (500 g) macaroni noodles, cooked according to the directions on the package
- **8** ○ 1 cup (250 mL) frozen peas

Macaroni and Cheese 63

MAKE IT!

Preheat the oven to 375° F (190° C). Grease a 9" x 13" (23 cm x 33 cm) baking pan with oil and set aside. Warm the milk over medium heat in a medium saucepan until it starts to steam. Do not boil.

In a large saucepan, melt the butter over low-medium heat.

Stir in the flour, using a wooden spoon, and cook for 2 minutes, continuing to stir. This is the roux.

Whisk the heated milk into the roux mixture and continue whisking until the sauce has thickened and is smooth. Bring to a boil.

Reduce the heat and continue simmering over low heat for about 5 minutes. Remove from the heat and add the grated cheddar cheese, salt and pepper.

Add the cooked pasta and peas: stir well.

7

Pour into the prepared baking dish. Bake in the oven for 30 minutes or until the top is starting to turn golden and the sauce is bubbling. Cool for a few minutes and serve.

Variations/Tips

- A roux can be used to make many sauces.
- The key to a good sauce is the cooking of the flour in the roux. If the roux isn't cooked enough, the sauce won't be as smooth as it should be and it will have a floury mouthfeel.

True Or False?

The cooked flour and butter base of the sauce, called the roux, is what makes a smooth sauce.

Answer

True: The starch granules in the flour swell up and absorb the liquid in the milk.

Macaroni and Cheese

Mango Mousse with Pineapple Jelly

let's make some!

We'll learn about enzymes!

Serves 6.
Adult needed: Yes
Hands-on time: 20 minutes
Total time: 3 hours 20 minutes

✓ YOUR CHECKLIST!

✓ KITCHEN GEAR

- Small saucepan
- Measuring cups
- Measuring spoons
- Large spoon
- 2 large bowls
- Hand mixer
- Rubber spatula
- Six 8 oz (250 mL) glasses or bowls
- Plastic wrap
- Food processor

✓ INGREDIENTS

1. 1/4 cup (60 mL) cold water
2. 2 Tbsp + 1 tsp (30 mL + 5 mL) unflavoured gelatin
3. 2 cups (500 mL) fresh mango purée (about 2 or 3 peeled and pitted mangos, the flesh puréed) or 3 cups (750 mL) unsweetened mango chunks, thawed from frozen and puréed
4. 1/3 cup + 1 Tbsp (80 mL + 15 mL) granulated sugar
5. 1 cup (250 mL) plain yogurt
6. 1 cup (250 mL) whipping cream
7. 1 cup (250 mL) pineapple juice

Mango Mousse with Pineapple Jelly

MAKE IT!

For instructions on how to make whipped cream by hand, see the Strawberry Shortcake recipe on page 86.

1 To make the mousse, place the water in a small saucepan.

2 Sprinkle 1 Tbsp (15 mL) plus 1 tsp (5 mL) gelatin over the water and let it soften for a minute or two. Heat the mixture over low heat, stirring often, until the gelatin is dissolved (the liquid will be clear). Remove from the heat.

3 Add the mangoes to a food processor, and pulse until smooth. Combine the puree, 1/3 cup (80 mL) sugar, and the gelatin mixture in a large bowl; mix well.

4 Stir in the yogurt until combined.

5 Place the whipping cream in a large, clean bowl. Whip the cream on high speed using a hand mixer until the cream forms stiff peaks.

6 Using a rubber spatula, fold the whipped cream into the mango mixture gently but thoroughly, until you can't see any more spots of cream.

Divide the mousse into six 8 oz (250 mL) glasses or bowls and cover with plastic wrap. Refrigerate the mousse for at least 2 hours or overnight.

To make the pineapple jelly, place the pineapple juice in a small saucepan.

Sprinkle 1 Tbsp (15 mL) gelatin over the juice and add 1 Tbsp (15 mL) sugar; let the gelatin soften for a minute or two. Heat the mixture over low heat, stirring often, until the gelatin is dissolved. Remove from the heat and let cool for a few minutes.

Pour the pineapple jelly mixture over the mango mousse, dividing the mixture evenly in the 6 glasses or bowls. Return to the refrigerator and chill for at least 1 hour. Serve cold.

Dear I.Q. . . . I'm in a puddle!

Q: I want to make yummy mango mousse that includes a topping of pineapple jelly. Yesterday, I tested out the dessert using fresh pineapple juice, and the gelatin just wouldn't hold together no matter how long I chilled it in the fridge!

— Puzzled over Pineapples in Pickering

Dear Puzzled,
Well, it's a fact that gelatin desserts are doomed when you add certain fresh fruits, like papaya, kiwi or pineapple, to the mix. The gelatin won't set and firm up if the enzyme bromelain in the pineapple breaks down the protein chains, keeping the gelatin liquid. But don't panic and skip the pineapple; there is a way to beat that enzyme, with science!

Heat changes the bromelain, breaking it down and taking away its enzyme power. So you could simmer your fresh pineapple juice to a temperature of 158 F (70 C) to deactivate the enzyme, then add it to the gelatin after it has cooled. Or, use canned pineapple juice — it's already been heated in the canning process and is easy to add.

Either way, I'm sure your pineapple gelatin topping the mango mousse will be exploding with flavour!

— Yours in food & science, I.Q.

Minestrone Soup

let's make some!

We'll learn about hemicellulose!

Serves 6.
Adult needed: Yes
Hands-on time: 15 minutes
Total time: 1 hour 30 minutes

✓ YOUR CHECKLIST!

✓ KITCHEN GEAR
- ○ Measuring spoons
- ○ Measuring cups
- ○ Large stock pot
- ○ Large spoon

✓ INGREDIENTS
1. ○ 1 Tbsp (15 mL) olive oil
2. ○ 1 cup (250 mL) thinly sliced leeks (just the white part)
3. ○ 1 cup (250 mL) diced carrots
4. ○ 1 cup (250 mL) diced onions
5. ○ 1 cup (250 mL) diced celery
6. ○ 1 cup (250 mL) diced peeled potato
7. ○ 1 28-oz can diced tomatoes
8. ○ 8 cups (2 L) water
9. ○ 1 Parmesan cheese rind (optional) — see bottom of next page
10. ○ 1 tsp (5 mL) fine sea salt or to taste
11. ○ 1 cup (250 mL) frozen peas
12. ○ 1/3 cup (80 mL) small pasta shape, such as stars or alphabet pasta
13. ○ 1 14-oz (414 mL) can cannellini beans, drained and rinsed

Minestrone Soup 71

MAKE IT!

1. Heat the olive oil in a large stock pot over medium heat. Add the leeks, carrots, onions, celery and potato.

2. Cook for about 5 minutes.

3. Add the diced tomatoes and water.

4. Add the Parmesan cheese rind, if using, and salt. Bring to a boil, reduce the heat to low and simmer for about 1 hour.

5. Add the peas, pasta and beans to the soup. Simmer for another 10 minutes or so. Remove the Parmesan cheese rind from the pot.

6. Taste the soup for seasoning. Serve hot.

What is a Parmesan cheese rind? When you buy a piece of Parmesan cheese, it often has part of the rind attached. Once you have grated the cheese, you are left with a hard rind that can be saved for adding flavour to soups. To keep a Parmesan rind until the next time you're making soup, wrap well in plastic wrap and freeze until needed.

Who can break down the walls?

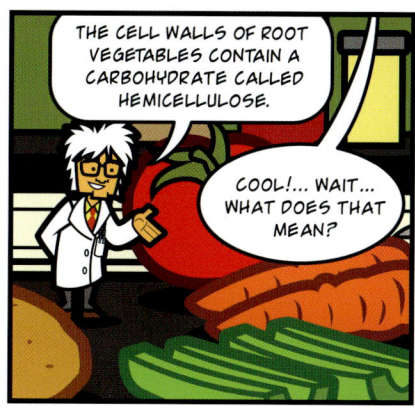
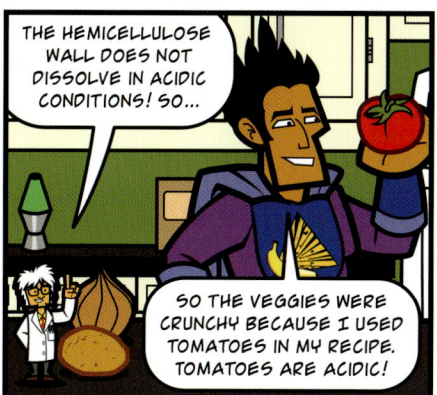

Minestrone Soup 73

Pickled Carrots and Dill Pickles

let's make some!

We'll learn about brine!

Makes 2 cups (500 mL).
Adult needed: Yes
Hands-on time: 15 minutes
Total time: Overnight

✓ PICKLED CARROTS

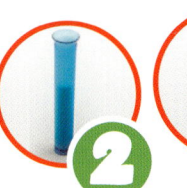

✓ KITCHEN GEAR

- Measuring cups
- Measuring spoons
- Microwave
- 1 pint (500 mL) glass canning jar
- Canning lid and ring

✓ INGREDIENTS

1. 3/4 cup (180 mL) rice wine vinegar
2. 2 Tbsp (30 mL) granulated sugar
3. 1 tsp (5 mL) kosher salt
4. 3 large carrots, peeled and cut into matchsticks
5. 1" (2.5 cm) piece of ginger root, peeled and thinly sliced

MAKE IT – PICKLED CARROTS!

1. Combine the vinegar, sugar and salt together in a small bowl and microwave until the sugar and salt have completely dissolved. Set aside.

2. Pack the carrots and ginger into the clean glass canning jar, filling it tightly.

3. Pour the prepared vinegar mixture over the carrots and ginger to cover. Add a little bit of water to the jar if the carrots at the top aren't covered with the vinegar.

4. Cover with a canning lid and ring. Refrigerate the pickles overnight before serving. Quick pickled carrots can be refrigerated in the canning jar for up to 1 week.

✓ DILL PICKLES

✓ KITCHEN GEAR
- ○ Measuring cups
- ○ Measuring spoons
- ○ Microwave
- ○ Large bowl
- ○ 1 pint (500 mL) glass canning jar
- ○ Canning lid and ring

✓ INGREDIENTS
1. ○ 3/4 cup (180 mL) white vinegar
2. ○ 2 Tbsp (30 mL) granulated sugar
3. ○ 2 tsp (10 mL) kosher salt
4. ○ 1/2 tsp (2 mL) mustard seeds
5. ○ 1/3 cup (80 mL) water
6. ○ 1 English cucumber, thinly sliced
7. ○ 1/3 cup (80 mL) coarsely chopped fresh dill
8. ○ 2 garlic cloves, coarsely chopped

MAKE IT — DILL PICKLES!

1. Combine the vinegar, sugar, salt, mustard seeds and water together in a small bowl. Microwave the mixture until the sugar and salt have dissolved.

2. Pack the cucumber slices, dill, and garlic into the clean glass canning jar, filling it tightly.

Pour the prepared vinegar mixture over the cucumbers to cover. Add a little bit of water to the jar if the cucumbers at the top aren't covered with the vinegar.

Cover with a canning lid and ring. Refrigerate the pickles overnight before serving. Quick dill pickles can be refrigerated in the canning jar for up to 1 week.

True or False?

Pickles keep from spoiling because they are packed in brine that draws water out of the vegetable cells.

answer

True: Pickles don't go off easily thanks to the salty water drawing most of the water out of the cells, leaving the pickles looking wrinkly and tasting yummy!

Pizza

let's make some!

We'll learn about gluten!

Serves 4 to 6.
Adult needed: Yes
Hands-on time: 15 minutes
Total time: 30 minutes

✓ YOUR CHECKLIST!

✓ KITCHEN GEAR
- ○ Large baking sheet
- ○ Parchment paper
- ○ Rolling pin (optional)
- ○ Fork
- ○ Brush
- ○ Knife or pizza cutter

✓ INGREDIENTS
1. ○ 1 ball pizza dough (store-bought), at room temperature
2. ○ All-purpose flour, for dusting
3. ○ Extra-virgin olive oil
4. ○ 1/2 cup (125 mL) pizza sauce (store-bought)
5. ○ Mozzarella cheese, freshly grated

✓ PIZZA TOPPINGS
6. ○ Thinly sliced pepperoni
7. ○ Finely chopped mushrooms
8. ○ Thinly sliced red peppers or whatever other pizza toppings you like

Pizza 79

MAKE IT!

1 Preheat the oven to 450° F (230° C). Line the baking sheet with parchment paper. Dust the surface of the dough with a little flour.

2 Using a rolling pin or your hands and a bit of flour, roll out the dough as thin as it will go.

3 Let the dough sit for a few minutes and go back to rolling it out if it is too elastic.

4 Place the dough on the prepared baking sheet. Press the dough out even more, creating a larger pizza surface. Poke the dough with a fork several times.

5 Brush with olive oil.

6 Sparingly distribute the pizza sauce over the dough.

80   Gastro Blast

Scatter the mozzarella cheese over the sauce.

Add any other toppings that you are using.

Place the pizza in the oven and bake for 10 to 15 minutes. Remove from the oven and let the pizza cool for a few minutes. Slice into wedges and eat warm.

Should I give gluten a break?

Gluten forms from proteins in the flour, making the dough stretchy. To be able to roll out the dough more easily, you need to:

a) Spin it in the air because it is fun.
b) Talk to the dough and tell it to chill out.
c) Let it rest in the fridge to let the gluten unwind.
d) Be a weightlifter.

answer
c) Let it rest in the fridge to let the gluten unwind.

Spaghetti with Tomato Sauce

Let's make some!

We'll learn about viscosity!

Serves 4.
Adult needed: Yes
Hands-on time: 15 minutes
Total time: 45 minutes

✓ YOUR CHECKLIST!

✓ KITCHEN GEAR
- Measuring spoons
- Measuring cups
- 2 large saucepans
- Large spoon
- 4 bowls for serving
- Ladle

✓ INGREDIENTS
1. 2 Tbsp (30 mL) olive oil
2. 1/2 cup (125 mL) finely chopped onions
3. 4 cups (1 L) puréed fresh tomatoes (or 4 cups [1 L] puréed canned tomatoes)
4. 4 basil leaves (or 1/4 tsp [1 mL] dried basil)
5. 1/2 tsp (2 mL) fine sea salt
6. 1/4 tsp (1 mL) freshly ground black pepper
7. 1 12 oz (340 g) package whole-wheat spaghetti noodles
- Grated Parmesan cheese, to serve (optional)

Spaghetti with Tomato Sauce

MAKE IT!

Boil water in a large saucepan and cook the pasta according to the package instructions.

Heat the olive oil in a large saucepan over medium heat. Add the chopped onions and cook until softened, about 5 minutes.

Add the puréed tomatoes and bring to a boil. Reduce the heat to low.

Add the basil leaves, salt and pepper and simmer for about 30 minutes.

Divide the spaghetti noodles into 4 bowls.

Ladle the tomato sauce onto the noodles and serve hot with a sprinkling of Parmesan cheese.

Don't let the doldrums win!

Strawberry Shortcake

let's make some!

We'll learn about liquids and solids!

Serves 8.
Adult needed: No
Hands-on time: 15 minutes
Total time: 1 hour 15 minutes

✓ YOUR CHECKLIST!

✓ KITCHEN GEAR
- ○ Measuring cups
- ○ Measuring spoons
- ○ Large bowl
- ○ Whisk
- ○ Spoon
- ○ Knife

✓ INGREDIENTS
1. ○ 4 cups (1 L) sliced fresh strawberries
2. ○ 1/3 cup (80 mL) granulated sugar
3. ○ 1 tsp (5 mL) pure vanilla extract
4. ○ 2 cups (500 mL) whipping cream
5. ○ 1/4 cup (60 mL) granulated sugar
6. ○ 8 Buttermilk Biscuits (recipe on page 8)

MAKE IT!

1. Combine the sliced strawberries, sugar and vanilla in a bowl.

2. Let sit for at least 1 hour at room temperature, stirring occasionally.

3. To make the whipped cream, place the cream in a large bowl.

4. Whisk the cream by hand until it starts to thicken slightly.

5. Add the sugar and continue whisking until soft peaks are formed.

6. Slice the biscuits in half and place the bottoms on individual plates.

Dollop about 1/2 cup (125 mL) whipped cream on the biscuit bottom.

Spoon about 1/2 cup (125 mL) sliced strawberries on the cream.

Place the top of the biscuit on the fruit and cream and serve.

Variations/Tips

· Instead of the strawberries, try using 4 cups (1 L) sliced fresh peaches, or a combination of blueberries, raspberries and strawberries (a combo known as "bumbleberry") equalling 4 cups.

· For instructions on how to make whipped cream using a hand mixer, see the Mango Mousse recipe on page 66.

True Or False?

Whipped cream makes a foam – a semi-solid.

Answer

True: Whip it too long and it becomes a solid, similar to butter; underwhip it and it reverts back to a liquid.

Stuffed Baked Potato Skins

let's make some!

We'll learn about starches!

Serves 4 to 8.
Adult needed: Yes
Hands-on time: 15 minutes
Total time: 1 hour 30 minutes

✓ YOUR CHECKLIST!

✓ KITCHEN GEAR
- ○ Large baking sheet
- ○ Vegetable scrub brush
- ○ Fork or potato masher
- ○ Knife
- ○ Large spoon
- ○ Large bowl
- ○ Brush

✓ INGREDIENTS
1. ○ 4 medium baking potatoes (Idaho or Russet potatoes are good)
2. ○ 1 tsp (5 mL) olive oil
3. ○ 1/2 tsp + 1/2 tsp (2 mL + 2 mL) fine sea salt
4. ○ 4 slices cooked bacon, diced
5. ○ 1 cup (250 mL) Greek yogurt
6. ○ 1/2 cup (125 mL) butter
7. ○ 1 tsp (5 mL) fine sea salt
8. ○ 1/2 tsp (2 mL) freshly ground black pepper
9. ○ 4 green onions, finely chopped
10. ○ 1 cup (250 mL) grated cheddar cheese

Stuffed Baked Potato Skins

MAKE IT!

Preheat the oven to 400° F (200° C). Scrub the potatoes clean. Dry thoroughly and brush each potato with a little olive oil. Sprinkle with salt and prick the potatoes in several spots with a fork.

Place the potatoes on the baking sheet and bake for about 1 hour. Remove from the oven and let cool until they are easy to handle.

Slice the potatoes in half lengthwise.

Carefully scoop the potato flesh out of the skins. Set the skins back on the baking sheet and place the flesh in a large bowl.

Combine all of the remaining ingredients — except the grated cheese — in a mixing bowl with the potato.

Mix well with a fork or potato masher.

Divide the filling mixture evenly into the 8 potato skins.

Sprinkle each filled potato skin with about 2 Tbsp (30 mL) grated cheddar cheese. Return to the oven and bake for 15 minutes or until the cheese is melted and the potatoes are hot.

One potato, two potato?

Potatoes that bake and mash easily:

a) Are weak and should exercise more.
b) Have the right balance of the two types of starch: more amylose than amylopectin.
c) Are too ripe.
d) Don't have enough starch.

answer

b) Have the right balance of the two types of starch: more amylose than amylopectin.

Sushi Vegetable Rolls

let's make some!

We'll learn about amylopectin!

Serves 2 to 3.
Adult needed: Yes
Hands-on time: 20 minutes
Total time: 1 hour

✓ YOUR CHECKLIST!

✓ KITCHEN GEAR
- ○ Measuring cups
- ○ Measuring spoons
- ○ Strainer
- ○ Medium saucepan
- ○ Small bowl
- ○ Medium bowl
- ○ Spoon
- ○ Bamboo sushi roller
- ○ Sharp knife
- ○ Platter

✓ INGREDIENTS
- **1** ○ 2/3 cup (160 mL) short grain brown rice
- **2** ○ 1 cup (250 mL) water
- **3** ○ 1 tsp + 1 tsp (5 mL + 5 mL) soy sauce
- **4** ○ 2 Tbsp (30 mL) rice wine vinegar
- **5** ○ 1/2 cucumber sliced into matchsticks
- **6** ○ 1/2 carrot sliced into matchsticks
- **7** ○ 1/2 red pepper sliced into matchsticks
- **8** ○ 1 green onion, finely sliced (green part only)
- **9** ○ 2 sheets nori (dried seaweed)
- ○ soy sauce, pickled ginger and wasabi, to serve (optional)

Sushi Vegetable Rolls

MAKE IT!

1. Place the rice in a strainer and rinse well under cold water. Shake the water out.

2. Place the rice in a medium saucepan with 1 cup (250 mL) water and 1 tsp (5 mL) soy sauce. Bring to a boil, cover, and reduce the heat to very low. Simmer for 40 minutes. Remove from the heat and let the rice sit, covered, for 10 minutes.

3. Combine 1 tsp (5 mL) soy sauce and the rice vinegar in a small bowl.

4. To prepare the sushi, place a bamboo sushi roller flat on a table. Sprinkle lightly with water. Place one nori sheet on top, smooth side down. With damp hands, press half of the rice flat on top of the nori, leaving 1 1/2 inches free of rice on edge farthest from you. Make sure the rice is pressed even and smooth.

5. Arrange half of the cucumber in an even strip horizontally across the rice, about 1 inch from the side closest to you. Lay half of the carrots, peppers and green onions in strips next to the cucumbers, creating a small bundle of vegetables.

6. To roll the sushi, beginning with the edge nearest to you, lift the sushi mat up with your thumbs, holding the filling in place with your fingers. Fold the mat/nori over the filling so that it becomes encased in the roll. Continue rolling the nori until it comes together in a tight roll. To serve, slice the ends off with a very sharp knife and slice each roll into 8 equal pieces.

Why so sticky?

Sushi Vegetable Rolls

Tossed Green Salad with 3 Salad Dressings

let's make some!

We'll learn about osmosis!

Serves 4.
Adult needed: No
Hands-on time: 10 minutes
Total time: 10 minutes

✓ YOUR CHECKLIST!

TOSSED GREEN SALAD

✓ KITCHEN GEAR
- Salad spinner
- Paper towels
- Large serving bowl
- Tongs
- Measuring cups

✓ INGREDIENTS
1 8 cups (2 L) salad greens (any one or a combination of several can be used) Some greens to try might be Romaine lettuce, Iceberg lettuce, Raddicchio, arugula, baby spinach or Boston leaf lettuce.

MAKE IT!

1 Tear the greens into bite sized pieces, and wash thoroughly. Dry in a salad spinner, or with paper towel. Place the greens in a large serving bowl. Drizzle about 1/2 a cup (125 ml) of salad dressing over the salad and toss with the tongs. Serve immediately.

EASY RANCH DRESSING

Makes about 1 1/2 cups (about 375 mL).

✓ KITCHEN GEAR
- ○ 1 pint (500 mL) Mason jar with lid and ring
- ○ Measuring cups
- ○ Measuring spoons
- ○ Knife

✓ INGREDIENTS
- ①○ 1/4 cup (60 mL) buttermilk
- ②○ 1/2 cup (125 mL) mayonnaise
- ③○ 2 Tbsp (30 mL) fresh lemon juice (bottled lemon juice is also fine)
- ④○ 1 Tbsp (15 mL) finely chopped fresh parsley
- ⑤○ 1 Tbsp (15 mL) finely chopped fresh chives
- ⑥○ Pinch of fine sea salt, to taste
- ⑦○ Pinch of freshly ground black pepper, to taste

SOY SAUCE VINAIGRETTE

Makes about 1 cup (250 mL).

✓ KITCHEN GEAR
- ○ 1 pint (500 mL) Mason jar with a lid and ring
- ○ Measuring spoons
- ○ Measuring cups
- ○ Ginger grater

✓ INGREDIENTS
- ①○ 3 Tbsp (45 mL) soy sauce
- ②○ 3 Tbsp (45 mL) rice wine vinegar
- ③○ 2 Tbsp (30 mL) toasted sesame oil
- ④○ 1 Tbsp (15 mL) maple syrup
- ⑤○ 1 Tbsp (15 mL) finely grated ginger
- ⑥○ 1/4 cup (60 mL) vegetable oil

SIMPLE VINAIGRETTE

Makes about 1 cup (250 mL).

✓ KITCHEN GEAR
- ○ 1 pint (500 mL) Mason jar with a lid and ring
- ○ Measuring cups
- ○ Measuring spoons
- ○ Knife

✓ INGREDIENTS
- ①○ 3/4 cup (180 mL) extra-virgin olive oil
- ②○ 1/4 cup (60 mL) red or white wine vinegar
- ③○ 1 Tbsp (15 mL) Dijon mustard
- ④○ Pinch of fine sea salt, to taste
- ⑤○ Pinch of freshly ground black pepper, to taste

MAKE THEM!

1. Combine all of the ingredients for the dressing you've chosen in a mason jar.

2. Put the lid and ring on the jar.

3. Shake until well mixed.

Variations/Tips

- To turn the ranch dressing into a dip, add 1/2 cup (125 mL) sour cream to the dressing, taste for seasoning and serve with sliced veggies.

Dear I.Q. . . . What's going on with this salad?

Q. My sisters and I got to help with supper last night by making the salad. So we mixed the lettuce up, then added the vinaigrette dressing to the lettuce, tossing them together, and then went to watch our favourite show: Gastro Blast, of course. By the time supper was on the table, we saw our green salad had gone from crispy to limp. Help I.Q., we don't find soggy salad funny at all!

— Wilted and Wondering in Waterloo

Dear Wilted,

Well, with cooking and science, timing is everything! Sometimes you want food to soak up a flavour over a long time, and sometimes too much time is going to wreck the texture of the food.

When it comes to salad, it's okay to add a yummy dressing, but you have to time it just right. If you add it and toss it right before you eat it, it coats all the leaves and allows all those delicious flavours blended in the vinaigrette to slide around. But if you let that dressing sit on the lettuce leaves for too long, the oil in the dressing works its way past the natural, waxy, protective layer that surrounds the leaves and will cause the leaves to wilt.

Next time, eat your salad right away and then watch your favourite show!

— Yours in food & science,
I.Q.

Tzatziki with Homemade Yogurt

let's make some!

We'll learn about bacteria!

Tzatziki
Makes about 4 cups (1 L).
Adult needed: No
Hands-on time: 15 minutes
Total time: 3 hours 15 minutes

Homemade Yogurt
Makes about 4 cups (1 L).
Adult needed: Yes
Hands-on time: 10 minutes
Total time: Overnight

✓ TZATZIKI

✓ KITCHEN GEAR
- 2 fine-meshed sieves
- 2 large bowls
- Paper towels
- Measuring cups
- Measuring spoons
- Grater
- Mixing spoon

✓ INGREDIENTS
1. 4 cups (1 L) homemade yogurt, recipe below (or 4 cups [1 L] store-bought plain yogurt or 2 cups [500 mL] Greek yogurt)
2. 2 medium English cucumbers, unpeeled and seeded
3. 2 Tbsp + 1 tsp (30 mL + 5 mL) fine sea salt
4. 2 Tbsp (30 mL) white wine vinegar
5. 1/4 cup (60 mL) freshly squeezed lemon juice (bottled lemon juice is also fine)
6. 2 Tbsp (30 mL) olive oil
7. 1 garlic clove, minced
8. 1 Tbsp (15 mL) minced fresh dill

✓ HOMEMADE YOGURT

✓ KITCHEN GEAR
- Candy or deep-fry thermometer
- Large saucepan
- Spoon
- Thermos
- Towels
- Bowl

✓ INGREDIENTS
1. 4 cups (1 L) whole milk
2. 3 Tbsp (45 mL) plain yogurt

MAKE IT— TZATZIKI!

1 If using homemade or store-bought plain yogurt, lay a fine-meshed sieve over a large bowl and line the sieve with a double layer of damp paper towels. Place the yogurt in the sieve and let drain for 3 hours. If you are using Greek yogurt, omit this step.

2 Grate the cucumber and toss it with 2 Tbsp (30 mL) sea salt; place in another sieve with double layer of paper towel and set it over another bowl. Let sit for 3 hours.

Transfer the thickened yogurt to a large bowl.

Squeeze as much liquid from the cucumbers as you can and add the cucumbers to the yogurt.

Mix in the rest of the ingredients, including 1 tsp (5 mL) sea salt.

Serve immediately or cover and refrigerate until needed.

MAKE IT – HOMEMADE YOGURT!

Heat the milk to 100° F (38° C) in a saucepan.

Add the yogurt and mix thoroughly.

Pour the mixture into a good thermos (or two). Put the lid on the thermos

Wrap the thermos in two or three hand towels. Set it in a warm, draft-free place overnight. Spoon the yogurt into a covered container and refrigerate for up to 1 week.

I thought bacteria was bad?

The lactobacillus bacteria in yogurt:

a) Is alive.
b) Is friendly to your intestines, and helps with digestion.
c) Is microscopic.
d) All of the above.

answer
d) All of the above.

Tzatziki with Homemade Yogurt 105

Vegetarian Sloppy Joes and Marinated Zucchini Salad

let's make some!

We'll learn about freezing!

Vegetarian Sloppy Joes
Serves 4.
Adult needed: Yes
Hands-on time: 30 minutes
Total time: Overnight

Marinated Zucchini Salad
Serves 4.
Adult needed: No
Hands-on time: 15 minutes
Total time: 15 minutes

✓ VEGETARIAN SLOPPY JOES

✓ KITCHEN GEAR
- ☐ Knife
- ☐ Airtight container
- ☐ Large bowl
- ☐ Medium bowl
- ☐ Whisk
- ☐ Large frying pan

✓ INGREDIENTS
1. ☐ One 15 oz (425 g) block firm or extra-firm tofu
2. ☐ 1 cup (250 mL) thinly sliced button mushrooms
3. ☐ 1 cup (250 mL) ketchup
4. ☐ 1 tsp (5 mL) Worcestershire sauce
5. ☐ 1 tsp (5 mL) balsamic vinegar
6. ☐ 1 tsp (5 mL) soy sauce
7. ☐ 1/3 cup (80 mL) molasses
8. ☐ 1 tsp (5 mL) chili powder
9. ☐ 2 garlic cloves, minced
10. ☐ 2 Tbsp (30 mL) olive oil
11. ☐ 1 cup (250 mL) finely chopped onion
12. ☐ 4 whole grain hamburger buns, split

✓ MARINATED ZUCCHINI SALAD

✓ KITCHEN GEAR
- ☐ Vegetable peeler
- ☐ Large bowl
- ☐ Spatula
- ☐ Small bowl
- ☐ Measuring spoons

✓ INGREDIENTS
1. ☐ 1 medium yellow zucchini
2. ☐ 1 medium green zucchini
3. ☐ 3 Tbsp (45 mL) freshly squeezed lemon juice (lemon juice is also fine)
4. ☐ 3 Tbsp (45 mL) extra-virgin olive oil
5. ☐ 1 garlic clove, minced
6. ☐ Pinch of fine sea salt, to taste
7. ☐ Pinch of freshly ground black pepper, to taste
8. ☐ 2 Tbsp (30 mL) finely chopped fresh parsley, mint, chives, dill, or a combination of any of these herbs

MAKE IT – VEGETARIAN SLOPPY JOES!

1. Drain the tofu and slice into 1/2 inch (1 cm) pieces. Place the pieces in an airtight container and freeze until solid, preferably overnight.

2. Thaw the tofu to room temperature. Squeeze each piece of tofu until all of the moisture is released.

Crumble the tofu using your fingers and place in a large bowl.

Add the sliced mushrooms. Set aside.

To make the sauce, combine the ketchup, Worcestershire sauce, balsamic vinegar, soy sauce, molasses, chili powder and minced garlic in a medium bowl.

Whisk until smooth.

Pour the sauce over the crumbled tofu and mushrooms and mix until everything is coated.

Heat the olive oil over medium heat in a large frying pan. Add the finely chopped onion and sauté until the onion is soft, about 5 minutes.

Add the tofu and mushroom mixture and cook, stirring frequently, for about 15 minutes.

To serve, place the hamburger buns on four plates. Divide the tofu mixture between the plates and serve warm with Marinated Zucchini Salad.

MAKE IT – MARINATED ZUCCHINI SALAD!

1 Using a vegetable peeler, slice the zucchinis in long, thin strips, creating ribbons. Place the zucchini ribbons in a large bowl.

2 Stir together the lemon juice, olive oil, minced garlic, sea salt and pepper in a small bowl.

3 Pour the vinaigrette over the sliced zucchini and toss gently with the fresh herbs.

4 Taste for seasoning and serve with Vegetarian Sloppy Joes.

True Or False?

Tofu can't be frozen since it wrecks the flavour.

answer

False: Many fruits' and vegetables' textures suffer when frozen, but freezing actually helps tofu to become even more spongelike and better able to absorb flavours.

Veggie Lasagna and Ricotta Cheese

let's make some!

We'll learn about acids!

Veggie Lasagna
Serves 8 to 10.
Adult needed: Yes
Hands-on time: 15 minutes
Total time: 1 hour

Ricotta Cheese
Makes about 2 cups.
Adult needed: Yes
Hands-on time: 10 minutes
Total time: 1 hour 15 minutes

✓ VEGGIE LASAGNA

✓ KITCHEN GEAR

- ◯ Measuring cups
- ◯ Measuring spoons
- ◯ Large spoon
- ◯ Medium bowl
- ◯ 9" x 13" (23 cm x 33 cm) baking dish
- ◯ Tinfoil

✓ INGREDIENTS

1. ◯ 1 bowl of grilled vegetables:
   2 Bell Peppers, 2 small zucchinis, 1 80 oz package (250 g) fresh mushrooms, all sliced and sauteed with 2 Tbsp (30 mL) olive oil, 2 gloves of garlic (minced), 1/2 tsp (2 mL) fine sea salt, 1/4 tsp (1 mL) freshly ground black pepper
2. ◯ 2 cups (500 mL) ricotta cheese (see recipe below or use store-bought)
3. ◯ 1 large egg, beaten
4. ◯ 1 cup (250 mL) grated Parmesan cheese
5. ◯ 8 cups (2 L) tomato sauce
6. ◯ 1 package no-boil lasagna noodles
7. ◯ 1 lb (454 g) mozzarella cheese, grated

✓ RICOTTA CHEESE

✓ KITCHEN GEAR

- ◯ Sieve or colander
- ◯ Paper towels
- ◯ Large bowl
- ◯ Measuring cups
- ◯ Measuring spoons
- ◯ Large heavy pot
- ◯ Large spoon
- ◯ Container

✓ INGREDIENTS

1. ◯ 8 cups (2 L) whole milk
2. ◯ 1 cup (250 mL) whipping cream
3. ◯ 1/2 tsp (2 mL) fine sea salt
4. ◯ 1/4 cup (60 mL) fresh lemon juice

MAKE IT – VEGGIE LASAGNA!

1 Combine the ricotta cheese, egg and Parmesan cheese in a medium bowl. Set aside.

2 Spread about 2 cups (500 mL) tomato sauce on the bottom of a 13" x 9" (33 cm x 23 cm) baking dish.

Veggie Lasagna and Ricotta Cheese

Arrange a single layer of noodles over the sauce.

Dollop half of the ricotta mixture on the noodles and spread with a spoon.

Layer 1/3 of the sautéed veggies on the ricotta layer.

Cover with 2 cups (500 mL) tomato sauce.

Put another layer of noodles and spread any remaining tomato sauce and veggies over everything.

Top with the grated mozzarella.

Cover with tinfoil and bake for about 35 minutes.

Remove the tinfoil and continue baking for another 10 minutes or until bubbling. Let the lasagna sit for at least 5 minutes before serving.

MAKE IT – RICOTTA CHEESE!

Line a sieve or colander with a damp paper towel and place on a large bowl; set aside. Rinse a large, heavy pot with water. Add the milk, cream and salt to the pot and stir. Slowly bring the mixture to a rolling boil over medium-high heat, stirring occasionally.

Add the lemon juice to the boiling mixture. Reduce the heat to low and stir constantly for about 2 minutes. The mixture should be separated into curds and whey (curdled).

Pour the mixture into the prepared sieve or colander and let it drain for about 1 hour. Spoon the ricotta into a clean container, cover and refrigerate for up to 2 days.

Can the cheese be saved?

Whole Wheat Bread

let's make some!

We'll learn about gluten!

Makes 1 loaf.
Adult needed: Yes
Hands-on time: 20 minutes
Total time: 4 hours

✓ YOUR CHECKLIST!

✓ KITCHEN GEAR

- ○ Measuring spoons
- ○ Measuring cups
- ○ Small bowl
- ○ Large bowl
- ○ Large greased bowl
- ○ Large spoon
- ○ Wooden cutting board
- ○ Plastic wrap
- ○ 8" x 4" (20 cm x 10 cm) loaf pan

✓ INGREDIENTS

- **1** ○ 2 Tbsp (30 mL) warm water
- **2** ○ 1 tsp (5 mL) granulated sugar
- **3** ○ 1 Tbsp (15 mL) active dry yeast (1 packet)
- **4** ○ 3 1/2 cups (875 mL) whole wheat flour, plus a little extra for the work surface
- **5** ○ 1 1/4 tsp (6 mL) fine sea salt
- **6** ○ 1 cup (250 mL) 2% milk
- **7** ○ 1/4 cup (60 mL) vegetable oil
- **8** ○ 1/4 cup (60 mL) honey

Whole Wheat Bread 117

MAKE IT!

1. Combine the warm water, sugar and yeast in a small bowl. Let sit for 5 minutes.

2. Add the milk, oil, honey, and the yeast mixture to a medium bowl.

3. Add the flour and the salt to the wet ingredients, and form a ball of dough.

4. Generously sprinkle some flour on the wooden cutting board. Knead the dough for about 10 minutes (see I.Q.'s letter on the next page for instructions).

Place the kneaded dough into a large greased bowl and cover loosely with plastic wrap. Set the bowl in a warm place to rise for 2 hours.

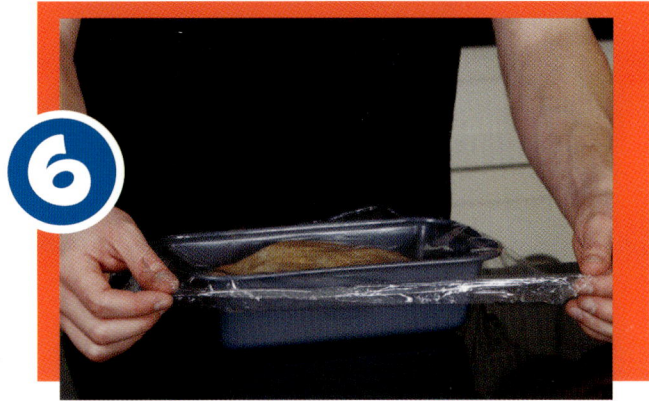

Grease the 8 x 4 inch (20 cm x 10 cm) loaf pan with oil. After the dough has risen, place the kneaded dough in the prepared pan and cover loosely with plastic wrap. Let the dough rise again for about 1 hour. Preheat the oven to 375 F (190 C). Remove the plastic wrap from the pan and bake the bread in the oven for about 40 minutes or until the bread is a dark golden brown on top and sounds hollow when tapped. Let the bread cool to room temperature, slice and serve.

Dear I.Q. . . . Do you need to knead?

Q: Our class wanted to find out what it was like to live as a pioneer, so we tried baking homemade bread at school. I always thought it came in a bag, so it was all new to me! Anyway, we each had a job to do, and mine was to take a turn kneading. Kneading was a lot of work and not so much fun, so I guess I skipped most of it.

When the bread came out of the oven, it smelled really good, but it was dense and hard to chew. Wow, the pioneers sure had it tough. Bad news if you did all that work and you ended up with tough bread! Set me straight, I.Q., did my shortcut lead to bread that just couldn't cut it?

— Bewildered by Bread in Bracebridge

Dear Bewildered,

Well, it can be hard work to knead, but it's a step you can't leave out when it comes to making bread by hand. The pioneers weren't doing it for fun, that's for sure, but whether they knew it or not, they did it for science!

To knead the bread dough, sprinkle a clean surface such as a kitchen counter with flour. Press the dough with the heel of your hand onto the floured surface and then pull the dough up and fold in half. Turn the dough a 1/4 turn and then repeat, pressing the dough with the heel of your hand. Continue these steps for approximately 10 minutes.

Kneading the bread works the proteins that are in the flour and mixes them together to make strands of something called gluten. Gluten is elastic-like and strong, acting like the muscles in the dough, helping to stretch and hold onto the air pockets in the dough as it rises and bakes. This makes the bread chewy and airy at the same time.

If you get another chance to make more bread, set a timer for about 10 minutes of kneading — you can do it! Or just knead away, but press into the dough every few minutes or so to check if it is stretchy and springs back. If it does, then you know the gluten is working for you and you're on the right road to light, fluffy bread.

— Yours in food & science,
I.Q.

index

a
Apple Oatmeal Pancakes, 4
avocados
  Guacamole, 54

B
bacon
  Stuffed Baked Potato Skins, 90
bacteria, 18-19, 105
Baked Tortilla Chips, 54
beans
  Minestrone Soup, 70
beef (ground)
  Empanadas, 34
biscuits (See Buttermilk Biscuits)
biscuits, sweet, 13
bread
  Chicken Fingers, 14
  French Onion Soup, 44
breads
  Chocolate Zucchini Bread, 26
  Whole Wheat Bread, 116
bumbleberry, 89
Buttermilk Biscuits, 8

C
cheese
  Parmesan cheese rind, 72
cheese
  French Onion Soup, 44
  Macaroni and Cheese, 62
  Stuffed Baked Potato Skins, 90
  Veggie Lasagna and Ricotta Cheese, 110
Chicken Fingers, 14
Chicken Pot Pie, 20
chicken stock
  French Onion Soup, 44
Chocolate Zucchini Bread, 26
cooking techniques
  flour a baking pan, 29
  hard boil eggs, 33
  knead bread dough, 119
  make a roux, 64, 65
  make buttermilk, 13
  make meringue, 60-61
  make yogurt, 104-105
  parboil vegetables, 25
  peel hard-boiled eggs, 33
  scoop an avocado, 56
  whip cream, 68

D
desserts
  Lemon Meringue Pie, 58
  Mango Mousse with Pineapple Jelly, 66
  Strawberry Shortcake, 86
Devilled Eggs, 30
Dill Pickles, 76
dough
  Buttermilk Biscuits, 8
  Empanadas, 34
  Pizza, 78
  Whole Wheat Bread, 116

e
Easy Ranch Dressing, 100
eggs
  Apple Oatmeal Pancakes, 4
  Chocolate Zucchini Bread, 26
  Devilled Eggs, 30
  Lemon Meringue Pie, 58
Empanadas, 34

F
Fish Tacos, 40
flour (wheat)
  Apple Oatmeal Pancakes, 4
  Buttermilk Biscuits, 8
  Chocolate Zucchini Bread, 26
  Empanadas, 34
  Whole Wheat Bread, 116
French Onion Soup, 44
fruit
  Apple Oatmeal Pancakes, 4
  Mango Mousse with Pineapple Jelly, 66
  Strawberry Shortcake, 86

G
Granola and Granola Bars, 48
Guacamole, 54

H
how to ... (See cooking techniques)

L
Lasagna (See Veggie Lasagna and Ricotta Cheese)
Lemon Meringue Pie, 58

M
Macaroni and Cheese, 62
Mango Mousse with Pineapple Jelly, 66
Marinated Zucchini Salad, 106
meat stock
  French Onion Soup, 44
Minestrone Soup, 70

n
noodles
  Macaroni and Cheese, 62
  Spaghetti with Tomato Sauce, 82
  Veggie Lasagna, 110

o
oats (rolled)
  Apple Oatmeal Pancakes, 4
  Granola and Granola Bars, 48
onions
  French Onion Soup, 44

P
pancakes (See Apple Oatmeal Pancakes)
Parmesan cheese rind, 72
pasta
  Minestrone Soup, 70
  Spaghetti with Tomato Sauce, 82
  Veggie Lasagna, 110
Pickled Carrots, 74
pickles
  Dill Pickles, 76
  Pickled Carrots, 74
pie (See Lemon Meringue Pie)
Pizza, 78
potatoes
  Stuffed Baked Potato Skins, 90

R
rice
  Sushi Vegetable Rolls, 94
Ricotta Cheese, 110

S
salad dressings
  Tossed Green Salad, 98
salads
  Marinated Zucchini Salad, 106
  Tossed Green Salad, 98
Simple Vinaigrette, 100
Sloppy Joes (See Vegetarian Sloppy Joes)
soups
  French Onion Soup, 44
  Minestrone Soup, 70
Soy Sauce Vinaigrette, 100
Spaghetti with Tomato Sauce, 82
stock (chicken or beef)
  French Onion Soup, 44
Strawberry Shortcake, 86
Stuffed Baked Potato Skins, 90
Sushi Vegetable Rolls, 94

T
techniques, cooking (See cooking techniques)
tofu
  Vegetarian Sloppy Joes, 106
tomato sauce
  Spaghetti with Tomato Sauce, 82
tortilla chips
  Guacamole, 54
tortillas
  Fish Tacos, 40
Tossed Green Salad, 98
Tzatziki with Homemade Yogurt, 102

V
vegetables
  Chicken Pot Pie, 20
  Fish Tacos, 40
  Marinated Zucchini Salad, 106
  Minestrone Soup, 70
  Pickled Carrots and Dill Pickles, 74
  Stuffed Baked Potato Skins, 90
  Sushi Vegetable Rolls, 94
  Tossed Green Salad, 98
  Veggie Lasagna and Ricotta Cheese, 110
Vegetarian Sloppy Joes, 106
Veggie Lasagna and Ricotta Cheese, 110

W
Whole Wheat Bread, 116

Y
yogurt
  Apple Oatmeal Pancakes, 4
  Fish Tacos, 40
  Mango Mousse with Pineapple Jelly, 66
  Stuffed Baked Potato Skins, 90
  Tzaziki with Homemade Yogurt, 102

Z
zucchini
  Chocolate Zucchini Bread, 26